PAGEANTRY & PERFORMANCE

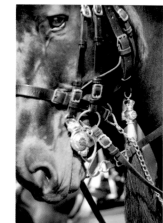

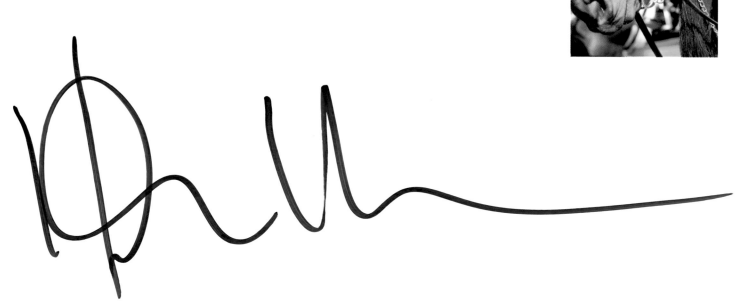

— DEDICATION —
TO THE HOUSEHOLD CAVALRY
AND ALL THE PEOPLE WHO APPRECIATE ITS ETHOS
AND SENSE OF PROUD TRADITION

PAGEANTRY & PERFORMANCE

THE HOUSEHOLD CAVALRY IN A CELEBRATION OF PICTURES

HENRY DALLAL

STRATEGIC REAL ESTATE ADVISORS

Preserving capital for the next generation

Pageantry & Performance
The Household Cavalry in a Celebration of Pictures

Written & Published by
Henry Dallal

Email: info@henrydallal.com
www.henrydallal.com

All Photographs by
Henry Dallal
and
Back flap & page 5, by Jessica Fulford-Dobson
Page 47, top left, by Helen Revington & Stephen Sparks

Design & Production
Sunita Gahir
www.bigmetalfish.com

Text Editors
Peter Ashman
Jamie Campbell
Col Hamon Massey

Jacket Text
Lady Olga Maitland

Reproduction by Reed Digital, Ipswich, Suffolk England
www.reeddigital.co.uk

Printed and bound in Italy by Grafiche Milani

ISBN 0 9544083 0 6

© Henry Dallal 2003

Reprinted: September 2003

My deepest gratitude to BAE Systems Plc *for their continuous*
and generous support in my photographic projects

BAE SYSTEMS

Acknowledgments

There are many people I should like to thank, and if I were to name them all, the list would be as long as a roll call of the regiment itself. However, it is very important to mention a few people for whose support, encouragement and guidance I am greatly indebted.

WO2 N. R. H. Peers, who first introduced me to this close community tucked away in the heart of Knightsbridge, has not only shared his knowledge of the regiment, its tales and procedures, but has also shed light on its many equine characters.

Many people in the Household Division and at the Headquarters of the Household Cavalry need to be mentioned, including: Maj Gen Redmond Watt; Maj Gen Sir Evelyn Webb-Carter; General the Lord Guthrie of Craigiebank as Colonel, The Life Guards and Gold Stick; Col Hamon Massey; Col Toby Browne; two commanding officers, Lt Col Mark Ridley and Lt Col Stuart Cowen; Lt Col J. S. Olivier; Maj Sebastian Miller; Capt George Cordle; Sgt Zak Russell; Maj Sandy Sanderson; Capt Chris Haywood; Capt Richard Waygood; Wo2 Mark Kitching; Capt Paul Maxwell; Harry Whitbread and Simon Saunders at Media Operations and all those in the Household Division who allowed me to photograph them at all hours. Outside the Division I'd like to thank: The Crown Equerry; Lt Col Sir Seymour Gilbart-Denham; Terry Pendry; Peter Ashman; Lady Olga Maitland and Lord Mark Birdwood. A very special thank you is owed to BAE SYSTEMS Plc, who became exceptionally supportive of this project; and, also Rotch Property Group; Crown NorthCorp; Financial Security Assurance; Terra Firma Capital Partners; Cyberview Technology Ltd, Chello and finally, Sunita Gahir of Bigmetalfish who has designed the book and Ken Webb of Worth Partnership.

I would also like to thank Lise Hutton and all my many friends, including Michael Aston, Ben Stephens, Vincent Tchenguiz, Edward Meir and Ron Roark who have had to put up with me and helped me throughout; my father who passed on to me his habit of photographing special moments; my mother who introduced me to horses way back when (and encouraged me from afar), Jean-Jacques Pergeant of the Berkeley Hotel, Richard Scotto of Kodak Presentations, Suzy Watt and Gregg Walsh of Crocodile Studios and Aubyn Crawford; L/Cpl Barney Ashworth and L/Cpl Doug Eames, all of whom helped make possible the multi-media show from which this book is derived.

As this book is coming to print, I know too that the challenge of capturing beautiful images of this fascinating enigma will never be complete. My collection will never be enough!

H. Dallal

Her Majesty the Queen, Colonel-in-Chief of the Household Cavalry and all seven regiments of the Household Division, with Tinkerbell, Peter Pan and Tiger Lily in an exclusive photograph taken for 'All the Queen's Horses', the Golden Jubilee tribute to Her Majesty at the Royal Windsor Horse Show on 18 May 2002. Tiger Lily and Peter Pan were bred from Tinkerbell in the Royal Mews.

Photograph taken and reproduced here by gracious permission of Her Majesty.

Introduction by Henry Dallal

London came alive for me early one morning during a visit to the United Kingdom. The cause was my first sight of the Household Cavalry's Watering Order an inspiring way to start a day. Since then I have learnt that this exercise dates back to the days of cavalry in the field, when at sunrise horses were ridden from camp to a watering hole to drink. The images and sounds that I saw that morning ignited a spark of fascination, one that still glows inside me even after six years of photography.

When I finally moved to London, I was invited to visit the home of the Household Cavalry Mounted Regiment in Knightsbridge. few of the shoppers heading for nearby Harrods or Harvey Nichols would egin to guess at the world that lies behind the high brick walls of the arracks. Here there is a completely self-contained village—home to 250 orses and 350 officers, soldiers and their families—where life revolves ntirely around horses, well-rehearsed drills and discipline.

The closer I looked, the more I realised what a rich and vivid world it as. Every detail on the uniforms and every piece of polished brass on the ddlery had a reason. Behind every minute detail there was a story—and e 350 years of the Household Cavalry's history was woven into crests, eepskin blankets, gold outfits and helmets, for display to visiting heads state or on ceremonial processions.

My challenge as a photographer has been to capture something of this mbolism, to convey a little of my own love of horses and their individual

ABOVE: Levi and Warrior, Knightsbridge

personalities, and to explore the intricacies behind the scenes. I feel very privileged to have been welcomed by everyone within the regiment over the years; to have been allowed to absorb the culture and the spirit; to have captured so many intimate moments through photography. I am lucky to be able to call so many of them my friends.

During my study of the regiment I recall vividly the occasion at four o'clock one morning, when the stables were full of men in overalls mucking out. I thought they were stable boys but soon realised that they were, in fact, the same troopers who were to perform later in the day. The atmosphere of those early hours seems far removed from the splendour of the parades when the crowds flock to catch a

glimpse of glamour and pageantr capture not only the spirit but als on behind the scenes. There is Household Cavalry that is shar newest recruit to the most senior focused, versatile and all of them and pride in what they do.

I was snapping away with my for the Queen's Birthday Parade see a group of officers in the thought it must be a distraction mounting horses for the parade watching a squadron of The

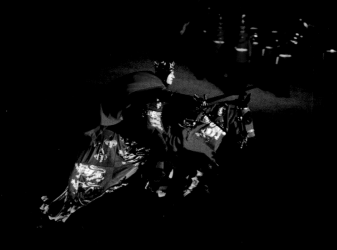

ABOVE: MAJ GEN REDMOND WATT, THE GENERAL OFFICER COMMANDING THE HOUSEHOLD DIVISION, INSPECTING THE ESCORT FOUND BY THE HOUSEHOLD CAVALRY (WITH A SQUADRON STANDARD OF THE BLUES AND ROYALS) AND THE FOOT GUARDS IN THE FRONT OF THE GUARDS MEMORIAL AT HORSE GUARDS ON THE MAJOR GENERAL'S REVIEW FOR THE QUEEN'S BIRTHDAY PARADE.

cautiously (in case of minefields) into Kosovo for the first time. In this group was General Sir Charles (now Lord) Guthrie, who as Chief of the Defence Staff at the time was responsible for the operation. He was present at Horse Guards on this day as the Colonel, The Life Guards and was about to ride down the Mall while the Kosovo story unfolded. Nothing could better demonstrate the dual role of the Household Cavalry: first and foremost, they are professional soldiers. Only after that are they ceremonial soldiers.

The following images give the reader a small glimpse into the life of the Household Cavalry — a few of the Household Division images are included as they come together in many ceremonials. The photographs can only scratch the surface of the history and tradition of the regiment although the coverage does include two of the major ceremonial events—the Queen Mother's funeral procession and HM The Queen's Golden Jubilee, both of which showed the very best of British spirit and style.

I hope that the next time you see the Household Cavalry on parade or a military operation you will think about all the hard work that has gone on behind the scenes as well as the rich tapestry of history, colour and tradition in the foreground. I have learned that one often does not always notice the jewels that lie on one's own doorstep; and this is a jewel that really sparkles. If I have allowed an ember of pride and appreciation to glow in the viewer at the beauty of this legacy of excellence, then I have succeeded.

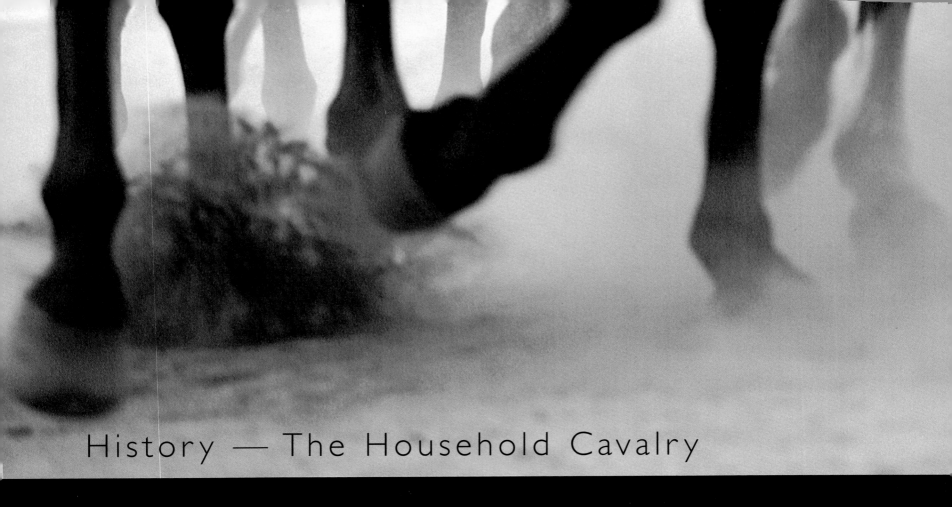

Ⓞn fine horses, resplendent in their highly polished cuirasses and gleaming helmets, the Household Cavalry is an indispensable part of the pageantry of royal Britain. It is hard to believe that these gloriously uniformed men are, first and foremost, professional soldiers in a crack corps made up of two regiments, The Life Guards and The Blues and Royals each split equally between the regiment at Windsor equipped for armoured reconnaissance and the Household Cavalry Mounted Regiment in London, equipped for mounted State and Royal ceremonial. Except for certain specialists, members of the Household Cavalry—Great Britain's two oldest and most senior cavalry regiments—have to be fully qualified in both roles. They must be able to perform their ceremonial mounted duties and then convert to their military speciality as part of an armoured unit: truly they are amongst the best of British!

Formed in 1660 by King Charles II, The Household Cavalry today comprises two regiments: The Life Guards and The Blues and Royals, the latter formed in 1969 from an amalgamation of The Royal Horse Guards

THE BATTLE HONOURS OF THE LIFE GUARDS START WITH DETTINGEN IN 1743. THE LAST—TO DATE—IS THE GULF 1991.

HRH The Princess Royal, Colonel The Blues and Royals at the Queen's Birthday Parade. To Her right, HRH the Prince of Wales and HRH the Duke of Edinburgh

(the Blues) and The Royal Dragoons (The Royals). The Household Cavalry's role today is what it was in 1660—close protection to the Sovereign through mounted escort—but the component regiments have always had a supreme fighting capability, as witnessed by their impressive list of battle honours, starting with that gained by The Royals at Tangiers (1662–80). Adaptability and versatility have always been bywords—popular imagination was stirred in 1882 by the moonlight charge of The Life Guards at Kassassin and the battle of Tel el Kebir, in Egypt. Since the end of World War II regiments of the Household Cavalry have seen service all over the world, including—in the last twenty years—the Falklands, the Gulf, Bosnia, Kosovo and Macedonia.

Her Majesty The Queen is Colonel-in-Chief, and each of the two regiments has a Colonel (appointed by the Sovereign), who also carries the title of Gold Stick. An appointment dating back to the reign of Charles II, Gold Stick is the closest military officer to the Sovereign with a badge of office in the form of an ebony staff with a gold head. The present Colonels are General The Lord Guthrie of Craigiebank GCB, LVO, OBE for The Life Guards, and HRH The Princess Royal KG, GCVO, QSO for The Blues and Royals. The Colonels are 'in Waiting' upon the Sovereign, alternating monthly, and are much involved in their Regiment's activities.

Next in seniority is Commander Household Cavalry and Silver Stick in-Waiting, a serving full colonel in the Household Cavalry, responsible to the two Gold Sticks for the day-to-day running of the Household Cavalry.

Early Morning Preparation

A very early start is necessary each morning to prepare horses for the Queen's Life Guard, and for the big parades. The horse must be saddled and bridled in the traditional manner which all takes time. Once this is done, the rider must spend more time getting himself dressed and ready for the rigorous inspection that inevitably follows. Early every morning the streets of London echo with the sounds of the Watering Order, which provides exercise for horses and riders not participating in the Queen's Life Guard that day.

TOP LEFT: PLANNING THE COMPOSITION OF THE QUEEN'S LIFE GUARD BY PAIRING UP HORSES AND RIDERS.

THE BLANKET RIDE.
TROOPERS ON THE
QUEEN'S LIFE GUARD THAT
DAY EXERCISE THEIR HORSES
WITH ONLY A BLANKET
INSTEAD OF A SADDLE
TO USE UP THEIR EXCESS
ENERGY PRIOR TO THEIR
PREPARATION, INSPECTION
AND DEPARTURE FOR
HORSE GUARDS.

HORSES LIKE HUMANS, CAN
BE HYPOCHONDRIAC,
OCCASIONALLY 'THROWING
SICKIES', (PRETEND TO BE ILL
TO AVOID THEIR DUTIES).

IT'S NOT THE EASIEST THING
IN THE WORLD, HAVING
FULL CONTROL OF THE
HORSE WHILE HANDLING
AND PLAYING A MUSICAL
INSTRUMENT, ENSURING
YOU'RE ON THE RIGHT
MUSIC SHEET AND, OH YES,
THERE'S A WHIP TOO!

EACH YEAR'S NEW HORSES
ARE NAMED ACCORDING TO
A LETTER OF THE ALPHABET.
SOME YEARS IT IS DIFFICULT
TO THINK OF THIRTY NEW
NAMES BEGINNING WITH
THE SAME LETTER.

THERE ARE 93 SEPARATE ITEMS OF BRASS WORK TO BE POLISHED BEFORE A SOLDIER GOES ON DUTY. FROM THE TIME HE TAKES A PAIR OF BRAND NEW JACK BOOTS OUT OF THE BOX, A SOLDIER WILL SPEND FIFTY HOURS 'BULLING AND BIFFING' (REGIMENTAL SLANG FOR POLISHING) WITH A JEWELLER'S CLOTH AND USE FOUR TINS OF POLISH TO GET THEM TO THE STANDARD REQUIRED TO GO ON PARADE.

The Household Cavalry's ceremonial uniforms are instantly recognisable: plumed helmets, colourful tunics, gleaming breastplates, shining swords, white gloves and highly polished jackboots. In the presence of royalty officers wear a gold cross belt instead of the usual white leather.

State trumpeters and musicians wear a gold State uniform (which

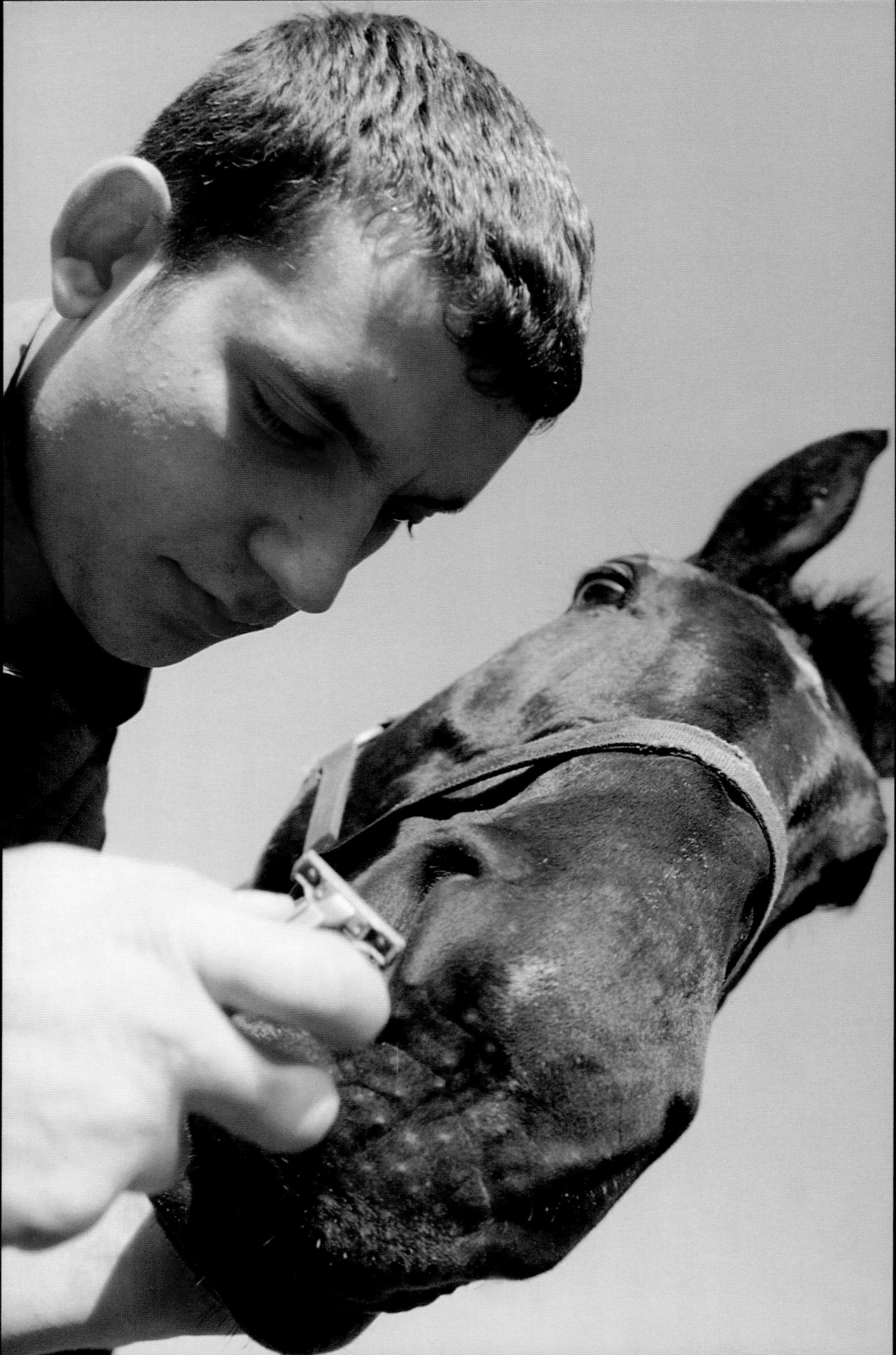

Horse Guards houses both HQ London District and Household Division as well as HQ Household Cavalry. It occupies the site that Henry VIII chose in 1533 for the construction of a tiltyard—where jousting competitions would take place. The tiltyard was later used by Queen Elizabeth I to stage two festivals— the anniversary of her accession and her birthday—a tradition reflected today with HM The Queen's Birthday Parade. The Household Cavalry provides two mounted sentries to guard the gate at Horse Guards, the official entrance to Buckingham Palace. The Queen's Life Guard is changed at Horse Guards daily at 11.00am (10.00am on Sundays). It is provided on alternate days by The Life Guards and The Blues and Royals. When the Sovereign is resident in London a Long Guard of an officer and 15 other ranks is mounted; a short guard of 12 men indicates that the Queen is not in London.

BELOW LEFT: View from
the sentry box at the
official entrance gate
to Buckingham Palace.
It's a varied scene as
tourists from all over
the world pass by.

'One morning, when I was part of the Queen's
Life Guard, a five-year old boy came up and
stood right next to my horse, looking up at me.
He was there with his mother, and he stayed
gazing at me for about a minute, and I didn't
budge. The mother turned to the boy and said,
"Don't worry, Tommy, he'll move in a minute."
That made me sit even more still, and after two
minutes I hadn't moved an inch. I could hear
the mother talking to her child again, more
impatiently this time: "Don't worry, Tommy,
he's bound to move in a moment, just hang
on." Well, after five minutes it was getting a little difficult to keep still—five minutes is a long
time when someone's right next to the horse,
watching you. So I peeked down at the lad. At
first all I could see was the top of his head, but
then I noticed that the horse was actually stand-
ing on one of his little sandals. The lad was
pulling away but his foot was pinned under the
horse's foot: he hadn't been interested in me at
all! So I kicked the horse a little, and she moved
over, and the mother and son wandered off.'

Capt R. Waygood, Riding Master

Since 1793, Hyde Park Barracks, on the edge of Hyde Park in Knightsbridge, has been home to approximately 250 horses and the men of the Household Cavalry, all of whom are active, professional soldiers. Within this barracks are also the specialist tradesmen who cater to the Regiment's needs, including farriers, saddlers and tailors. The entrance 'pediment' (see page 13) to the present barracks came from the riding school of the 1880 barracks.

PREVIOUS DOUBLE PAGE AND ABOVE: CONSTANT DRILLS IS A REGULAR SITE AROUND HYDE PARK BARRACKS

RIGHT: BASRA LOOKING SUSPICIOUSLY AT SADDLER L/COH WOOD DURING A FITTING SESSION.

The Farriers

TWICE A WEEK THEY INSPECT EVERY HORSE ON CAMP LOOKING FOR WEAR AND TEAR ON THE CAREFULLY 'MANICURED' HOOVES.

THE FARRIER'S AXE HAD TWO
FUNCTIONS: THE SPIKE WAS
USED TO PUT SEVERELY
INJURED HORSES OUT OF
THEIR MISERY, AND THE BLADE
WAS USED TO CHOP OFF THE
DEAD HORSE'S NUMBERED
HOOF. THIS WAS RETURNED
TO THE QUARTERMASTER'S
DEPARTMENT BEFORE A NEW
HORSE COULD BE ISSUED.

The Riding Master

The Riding Master plays a very important role in The Household Cavalry, being responsible for the training of horses and riders, and certain other equestrian matters.

LEFT: ONE NOTEWORTHY FIGURE IN THE ANNALS OF THE HOUSEHOLD CAVALRY IS MAJ WALTER L. THOMPSON, MVO, MBE, DCM WHO JOINED THE REGIMENT IN 1933, AND WAS INVOLVED IN ALL EQUESTRIAN MATTERS UNTIL THE OUTBREAK OF WAR. HE RECEIVED THE DCM, FOLLOWING ACTION IN BELGIUM IN 1940 AND IN 1945, SUPERVISED THE TRAINING OF HORSES AND SOLDIERS TO ESTABLISH FOR THE FIRST TIME A COMPOSITE REGIMENT AT KNIGHTSBRIDGE IN THE PRESENT FORM. HE WAS RIDING MASTER FROM 1952 UNTIL 1966, AT WHICH TIME HE WAS SUCCEEDED BY LT COL ALEC JACKSON, WHO WAS RIDING MASTER FOR THE NEXT 18 YEARS. A FINE HORSEMAN, MAJ THOMPSON ENTERED THE VERY FIRST THREE-DAY EVENT AT BADMINTON IN 1949, BECOMING THE FIRST HOUSEHOLD CAVALRYMAN TO COMPETE IN MILITARY UNIFORM (ALBEIT MINUS HARD HAT—NOT OBLIGATORY IN THOSE DAYS). HE COMPETED REGULARLY AND WAS THIRD IN 1951.

AFTER LEAVING THE ARMY, MAJ THOMPSON BECAME DRIVER AND INSTRUCTOR (COACH AND FOUR HORSES) TO HRH THE DUKE OF EDINBURGH FOR NINE YEARS, BEFORE HE BECAME A MILITARY KNIGHT OF WINDSOR.

BEAUFORT STAIRCASE

LEFT: CAPT RICHARD WAYGOOD BECAME RIDING MASTER IN 2002. HE'S SEEN HERE AT BADMINTON EARLIER IN THE YEAR JUMPING DOWN THE BEAUFORT STAIRCASE — A NOTORIOUS OBSTACLE.

BELOW: HER MAJESTY THE QUEEN WITH HER OWN HORSE PETER PAN. THE HORSE AT THIS TIME IS ON LOAN TO CAPT WAYGOOD WHO IS TRAINING HIM FOR THREE-DAY EVENTING.

'I joined the Household Cavalry as a trooper in 1979, and right from the start my dream was to be part of the Blue Mafia (as the equitation instructors are affectionately known) and to ride at Badminton, in uniform. In 2002 more dreams came true than I could have hoped for: I was the first military rider at Badminton in 22 years, I picked up the job of Riding Master, I led the Life Guard half of the Sovereign's Escort at the Trooping the Colour, and had the privilege of being out at the front of the marching party at The Queen Mother's funeral. And, to top it all, I rode Peter Pan— The Queen's horse—at Smiths Lawn, Windsor and at Gatcombe, coming first at both. A perfect year for me.'

Capt R. Waygood, Riding Master

Kit Ride Pass Out Parade—the parade that marks the end of a soldier's training when he is ready to take his place on parade and Queen's Life Guard duty. A special ceremony takes place in the Barracks in front of the Commanding Officer. Parents and friends of the 'graduating' trooper are invited and the Band of The Life Guards plays. It's a proud moment for the new trooper.

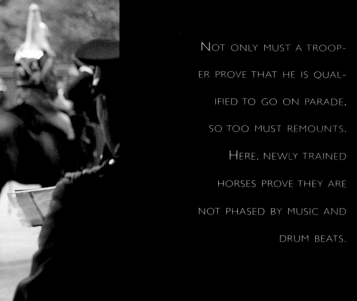

NOT ONLY MUST A TROOP-
ER PROVE THAT HE IS QUAL-
IFIED TO GO ON PARADE,
SO TOO MUST REMOUNTS.
HERE, NEWLY TRAINED
HORSES PROVE THEY ARE
NOT PHASED BY MUSIC AND
DRUM BEATS.

The State Visit

Windsor Castle was built by William I in 1067 but has seen many changes since then. The principal residence of the monarchs of England since the 14th century, it is regularly used for State occasions.

LEFT: REAVLY, ON THE STATE VISIT OF THE PRESIDENT OF GERMANY, JOHANNES RAU, DECIDES TO HAVE HIS OWN PARADE AS HER MAJESTY THE QUEEN'S CARRIAGE PASSES BY.

TROT PAST IN THE QUADRANGLE AT WINDSOR CASTLE FOR THEIR MAJESTIES KING ABDULLAH AND QUEEN ALIA OF JORDAN DURING THEIR STATE VISIT IN 2001.

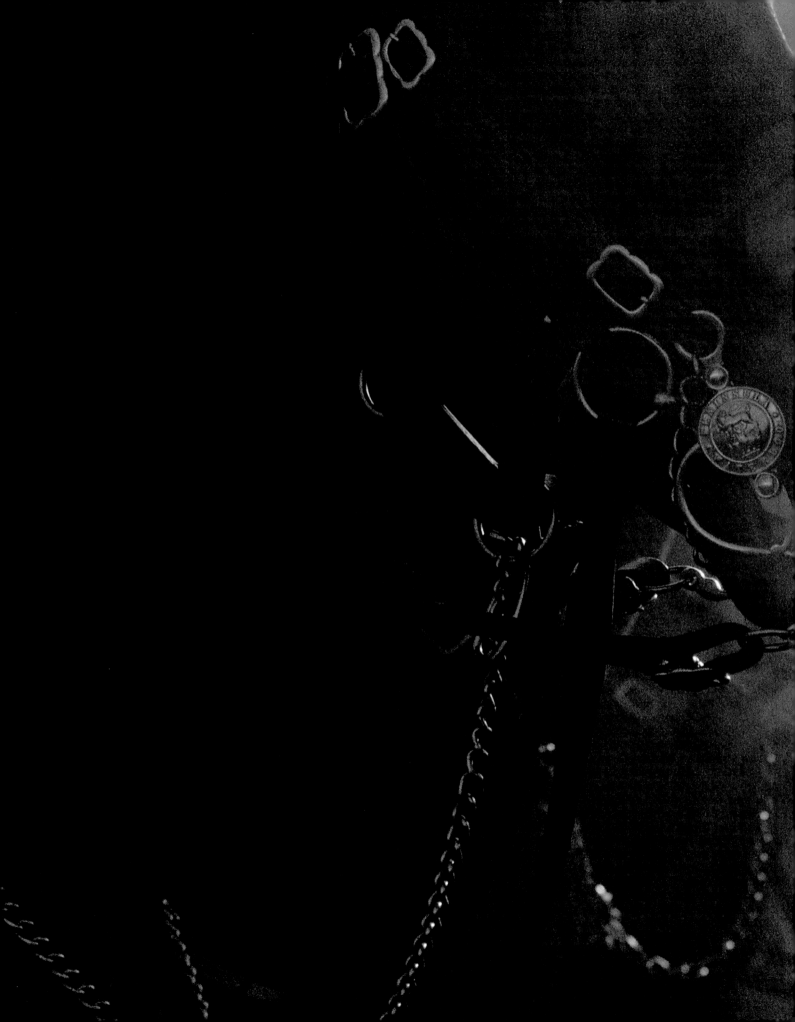

The annual inspection each April by the General Officer Commanding the Household Division signals the start of the summer parade season. The inspection is to ensure that the whole regiment is ready for the coming season.

RIGHT: IN BATTLE, THE CAVALRY RELIED UPON TRUMPET CALLS FOR COMMUNICATION BETWEEN THE COMMANDING OFFICER AND HIS TROOPS.

The Household Cavalry Musical Ride was first performed at The Royal Tournament in 1882. Based on a series of cavalry drill movements with the lance set to music. A highlight is when four men get their horses to lie down, and stay down, at their command—something that takes months of practice to perfect.

'There is no pressure, no adrenalin rush quite like what I felt at the Queen's Birthday Parade. I had to turn a heavy horse virtually on the spot, whilst starting the rolls on the kettle drums to begin the music of the Mounted Band. Any slight mistake will be noticed, and there are plenty of people there to do the scrutinising: the Royal Family, the Prime Minister, my parents and friends, the thousands in the crowd and countless others watching the TV. The nerves are unbearable, almost as bad if not worse than jumping out of a plane for the first time when training for parachuting. And the sense of relief unbelievable when, in a matter of minutes, it's all over.'

L/CoH Paul Kent

LEFT: L/CoH PAUL KENT ON JANUS HAS TO CONCENTRATE ON THE DRUM BEAT WHILE MAINTAINING THE TEMPO OF THE GAIT OF THE HORSE THAT LEADS THE PARADE. WHILST PLAYING THE DRUMS, HE HAS TO CONTROL THE HORSE ENTIRELY WITH HIS FEET VIA STIRRUP REINS, AS NO VERBAL OR CONVENTIONAL REIN SIGNALS ARE POSSIBLE.

RIGHT: OFFICERS SHARE A PRIVATE MOMENT. BEHIND THE GROUP, ON THE GROUND, CAN BE SEEN A SWORD, A LANCE AND A REVOLVER, USED IN A DISPLAY OF SKILL AT ARMS, A TEST OF HORSEMANSHIP AND MARKSMANSHIP.

The Combined Cavalry Memorial Parade takes place in Hyde Park each May to remember those of all cavalry regiments who have given their lives in the service of their Sovereign and Country since World War I. More recently, the main parade has been followed by Household Cavalry tributes paid at the nearby site of the memorial to the four men and seven horses killed in the IRA bomb outrage of 1982. To this day, as a mark of respect, each time the Queen's Life Guard passes the spot, they bring their swords to the carry, and 'eyes left' or 'eyes right' is given. Bands passing the scene stop playing as they near the spot, and resume once they have passed.

LEFT: MEMORIAL TO THOSE KILLED AND INJURED IN HYDE PARK BY THE IRA IN JULY 1982.

BELOW: HRH THE PRINCE OF WALES, TAKING THE SALUTE AT THE PARADE.

'I had seven months of gruelling training after joining the army; and then the Jubilee was upon us. But on top of that I wanted to take part in the Princess Elizabeth's Cup as a junior trooper; it took me nine days to get prepared. The jackboots themselves take three days to polish up. Everything has to be immaculate: frankly, you can't get any better than the standard out there. I managed to finish third and then, two weeks after that, I was one of only four Life Guards in the Retinue Party at Trooping the Colour, right behind The Queen. The preparation is hard, but it's worth it and I will do it again next year. You're so busy you don't even have time to think about it.'

Trooper Ivon Blevins

ABOVE: THE SOVEREIGN'S ESCORT AND MASSED BANDS FOR THE QUEEN'S BIRTHDAY PARADE

LEFT: THE PRINCESS ELIZABETH'S CUP IS AWARDED TO THE TROOPER JUDGED TO BE BEST TURNED OUT, IN FULL STATE UNIFORM, OVER THE PRECEDING YEAR. THE PICTURE SHOWS HM THE QUEEN DURING THE AWARD.

The Queen's Birthday Parade

LEFT: HER MAJESTY THE QUEEN AND HRH THE PRINCESS ROYAL, COLONEL THE BLUES AND ROYALS.

RIGHT: THE COLOUR PRESENTED BY THE QUEEN EARLIER IN THE YEAR TO THE SCOTS GUARDS, BEING DIPPED TO HER MAJESTY DURING THE QUEEN'S BIRTHDAY PARADE 2002.

FOLLOWING PAGE: THE MASSED BANDS OF THE GUARDS DIVISION PERFORM THE VERY INTRICATE SPIN WHEEL, AN EXTREMELY COMPLEX DRILL MANOEUVRE DEVISED TO ALLOW THEM TO CHANGE DIRECTION WITHOUT CHANGING FORMATION.

RIGHT: HRH PRINCE PHILIP, COLONEL, GRENADIER GUARDS AND THE RETINUE RIDE THROUGH THE GATES OF BUCKINGHAM PALACE TO THE COLONEL'S REVIEW N 2001. HE IS RIDING PHILLIPA, HIS FAVOURITE CHARGER. TO HIS RIGHT IS TERRY PENDRY, THE QUEEN'S STUD GROOM, RIDING ST JAMES THE HORSE WHICH THE PRINCE OF WALES WILL RIDE ON THE DAY OF THE QUEEN'S BIRTHDAY PARADE. ST JAMES WAS PRESENTED TO HER MAJESTY BY THE ROYAL CANADIAN MOUNTED POLICE. HER MAJESTY RECIPROCATED ON HER GOLDEN JUBILEE STATE VISIT TO CANADA BY PRESENT-ING GOLDEN JUBILEE, A FOUR-YEAR-OLD IRISH SPORTS HORSE TO THE RCMP. BEHIND HRH PRINCE PHILIP ARE THE COMPTROLLER, THE LORD CHAMBERLAIN'S OFFICE, THE MASTER OF THE HORSE (IN FEATHERS) AND THE CROWN EQUERRY.

The Queen's Birthday Parade is the most important parade of the year, dating as far back as 1700 when colours were rallying points in battle. The entire Household Division takes part, including the Household Cavalry, the five regiments of Foot Guards, (Grenadier, Coldstream, Scots, Irish and Welsh Guards), and the King's Troop, Royal Horse Artillery. There are three parades (the first two being rehearsals)—the Major General's Review, the Colonel's Review and finally HM The Queen's Birthday Parade.

Her Majesty The Queen surrounded by members of the Household Division including HRH the Duke of Edinburgh, Colonel Grenadier Guards; HRH the Prince of Wales, Colonel Welsh Guards; Maj Gen C. R. Watt, Maj General Commanding the Household Division and GOC London District, HRH The Princess Royal, Colonel The Blues and Royals. All are returning to Buckingham Palace after the Queen's Birthday Parade in 2001.

The Dismount

The parade continues behind closed doors back in Hyde Park Barracks, with the Regimental Dismount. A well choreographed display of synchronized motion of over a hundred horses and men is performed. The sound of the swords returning to scabbards simultaneously demonstrates an elegance of precision that stirs the heart. Only after the horses are turned in is the parade finally over. "Horses first, soldiers next, officers last!"

The Garter Ceremony

RIGHT: STATE TRUMPETERS— THE BANNERS ON THEIR TRUMPETS FEATURE THE ROYAL COAT OF ARMS AND THE ROYAL CYPHER.

LEFT: ON THE ROUTE FROM THE CASTLE TO ST GEORGE'S CHAPEL THE HOUSEHOLD CAVALRY PROVIDES A STAIRCASE PARTY AND STREET LINERS WITHIN THE GROUNDS OF WINDSOR CASTLE.

Founded by King Edward III in the early fourteenth century, the Most Noble Order of the Garter is the senior and most prestigious order of knighthood in the United Kingdom, consisting of members of the Royal Family and a limited number of knights companion, who join the order at the specific invitation of the Sovereign. The ceremony at which they join is very colourful, full of pomp and tradition. It takes place on the Monday following the Queen's Birthday Parade. Knights of the Garter gather at Windsor Castle, where new knights take the oath and are invested with the insignia of the order—the garter, star, riband, collar and mantle. This takes place in the twelfth century Garter Throne Room, followed by a service in St George's Chapel.

THE SILVER KETTLEDRUMS OF THE LIFE GUARDS (EACH WEIGHS 80LB/36KG) WERE PRESENTED TO THE REGIMENT BY KING WILLIAM IV IN 1832. THOSE OF THE BLUES AND ROYALS WERE PRESENTED BY KING GEORGE III IN 1805. ON PARADE, THE DRUMS ARE DRAPED WITH BANNERS, BEARING THE ROYAL COAT OF ARMS AND THE ROYAL CYPHER.

WINDING DOWN AFTER
ANOTHER PARADE—
MAJ D. ROBERTSON,
DIRECTOR OF MUSIC OF THE
BAND OF THE BLUES AND
ROYALS, WITH HIS HORSE
CONSTANTINE AND FRIEND.

*The Household Cavalry Regiment has
two bands, those of The Life Guards
and The Blues and Royals, both of
which have antecedents dating back
to 1660. As well as being fine
musicians and horsemen (usually proficient on
more than one instrument), they are also trained as
medical orderlies. They are involved in most state
functions and ceremonies, as well as performing in
concerts throughout the world.*

'We represent our country, and we do so on a daily basis. Most people don't realise that we have an armoured reconnaissance as well as a ceremonial regiment, and that they're entwined. Everyone in our regiment can perform operational duties one moment, and ceremonial duties the next. We don't just look good—we're fighters too.'

RCM Mark Kitching

Annual Training

Following a busy parade season, the Mounted Regiment leaves Knightsbridge in late August for annual training in Norfolk, where the men and their horses live 'under canvas' for three weeks. While there they perfect riding skills, compete in various competitions and engage in many outdoor training activities. This is a popular event in the calendar, allowing horses and riders to work together without the rigours of ceremonial duties. During annual training, the King's Troop, Royal Horse Artillery, takes over the honour of mounting the Queen's Life Guard.

Of all the parades during the year, the State Opening of Parliament is author Henry Dallal's favourite. The Household Cavalry plays a big role in the procession, which is very colourful, rich in pageantry, and usually carried out in beautiful autumn light. The atmosphere is electric and the noise—a thunderous combination of 200 or so horses, the clanging of swords and brass—powerfully unique, particularly when the parade goes through an arch- way or the echoes reverberate around a quadrangle.

State Opening of Parliament

The ceremony is held in the House of Lords, to which the Commons are summoned to hear the Sovereign's speech from the throne, setting out Government policies, and formally opening the next session of Parliament.

*The Sovereign travels to Westminster in a State Coach
drawn by four horses, with a Sovereign's Escort of
Household Cavalry. As the Queen arrives at the Sovereign's
Entrance to the House of Lords, the Royal Standard is
unfurled on the Victoria Tower, and it stays flying while The
Queen is within the Palace of Westminster. As The Queen
moves up the staircase to the robing chamber, she passes
between two lines of dismounted troopers of the Household
Cavalry, in full dress with drawn swords—one of the
occasions when they provide a Staircase Party and exercise
their privilege of being the only troops allowed to bear arms
within a royal palace.*

Christmas at Hyde Park Barracks

ABOVE: GENERAL THE LORD GUTHRIE OF CRAIGIEBANK, COLONEL THE LIFE GUARDS, HANGS THE BRICK AT HYDE PARK BARRACKS, DECEMBER 2001. ONE EXPLANATION FOR THIS RECENT LIFE GUARD TRADITION, STARTED IN 1889 IS AS FOLLOWS. JOE HOLLAND, A CIVILIAN FORAGE MASTER, WAS ABOUT TO JOIN NCOS FOR A CHRISTMAS DRINK. ON THE WAY, HE WAS SUMMONED TO GO INSTEAD TO JOIN THE COMMANDING OFFICER FOR SHERRY, SO HE THREW A BRICK ONTO A SLOPING ROOF, SAYING THAT HE WANTED THE MESS BAR TO REMAIN OPEN WHILE THE BRICK STAYED UP. HOURS LATER, HAVING SOBERED UP, HE DASHED BACK INTO BARRACKS TO FIND THE MESS BAR STILL OPEN FOR HIM. NOWADAYS, A BRICK IS CEREMONI-ALLY 'HUNG' ABOVE THE MESS BAR HERALDING THE BEGIN-NING OF THE CHRISTMAS FESTIVITIES.

ABOVE AND ABOVE RIGHT: GUESTS AND REVELLERS INCLUDE FORMER COMRADES, EXTENDING TO SOME FROM THE ROYAL HOSPITAL CHELSEA.

ABOVE RIGHT: A TRADITION ON CHRISTMAS DAY AT HYDE PARK BARRACKS IS FOR THOSE FORMING THE QUEEN'S LIFE GUARD TO TAKE PART IN AN EXTRA (AND EARLIER) PARADE— IN FANCY DRESS.

TOP RIGHT: MAX AND CONSTANTINE LOOKING ON CURIOUSLY AS THE SOLDIERS AND THEIR FAMILIES GATHER IN THE STABLES FOR A TRADITIONAL CHRISTMAS CAROL SERVICE.

ABOVE: THE QUEEN'S LIFE GUARD, MOUNTED BY THE BLUES AND ROYALS, FORMS UP AS THE LIFE GUARDS SLOW-MARCH THROUGH HORSE GUARDS IN THE FUNERAL PROCESSION FOR THE FIRST TIME IN 39 YEARS. ONLY ON SUCH OCCASIONS DO THE HOUSEHOLD CAVALRY MARCH IN DISMOUNTED REVIEW ORDER WITH SWORDS REVERSED.

LEFT: LT COL H.S.J. SCOTT, IN THE ANTE-ROOM AT WESTMINISTER PALACE, REFLECTS THE SOLEMNITY OF IT ALL

'...Almost immediately I was plunged into the thick of it. The Queen Mother passed away and everyone was completely stunned. We had to prepare for the ceremonial duties, but because we hadn't had a State

The Golden Jubilee

'I'd always wanted to be in the Army, but also wanted to work with horses. When I saw a picture of the Household Cavalry, I didn't have to think twice! I joined in 2001, and had less than eight months training before I was assigned to the Queen's Life Guard. At the moment we passed Buckingham Palace for the first time to give a salute and an "eyes right", my heart was pounding and I felt incredibly proud. Shortly afterwards I was out in front of the public for the Jubilee celebrations. There will only be one Golden Jubilee in my lifetime; and I can honestly say that to take part in it this year was the proudest thing I've ever done or will do. You can imagine that for a young lad from Northern Ireland who's never seen anything like this before, it was pretty special. That was the most powerful feeling I'll ever experience.

Thousands of people there, every one of them watching us; flags being waved, unbelievable cheering. And on top of this, to know that the Queen was following me ... words can't describe it. Everyone would have gladly given his right arm just to take part in that day. In years to come, I'll tell my children, and they in turn will tell their grandchildren that I took part in the Golden Jubilee.'

Tpr Ivon Blevins

MAJ SIR MICHAEL PARKER, MAJ GEN SIR EVELYN WEBB-CARTER AND GSM 'PERRY' MASON URGE THE HOUSEHOLD CAVALRY TO GET INTO POSITION DURING AN EARLY MORNING REHEARSAL FOR THE QUEEN MOTHER'S 100TH BIRTHDAY CELEBRATIONS. OTHER MILITARY SPECTACULARS SUCH AS THE GOLDEN JUBILEE CELEBRATIONS, AND 'ALL THE QUEEN'S HORSES' ARE PRODUCED AND CHOREOGRAPHED BY MAJ SIR MICHAEL PARKER. THE MAJOR GENERAL ALLOCATES THE HOUSEHOLD DIVISION TROOPS REQUIRED AND THE GARRISON SERGEANT MAJOR WORKS OUT THE DETAIL ON THE GROUND OF EACH MAN'S POSITION, DOWN TO MARKING IT WITH CHALK.

FOR 15 YEARS, UNTIL HIS RETIREMENT IN JULY 2002, THE POST OF GARRISON SERGEANT MAJOR, LONDON DISTRICT, WAS HELD BY WO1 (GSM) A. G. ('PERRY') MASON, MBE, MVO, COLDSTREAM GUARDS. GSM MASON, A LEGENDARY FIGURE WHO STOOD OVER SEVEN FEET TALL IN HIS BEARSKIN CAP, MARKED EVERY POSITION FOR EVERY HOUSEHOLD DIVISION SOLDIER FOR THE ENTIRE ROUTE OF THE GOLDEN JUBILEE PROCESSION FROM BUCKINGHAM PALACE TO ST PAUL'S CATHEDRAL WITH CHALK TO ENSURE THAT ALL WENT WELL ON 4 JUNE 2002.

THE GOLDEN JUBILEE MEDAL, PAID FOR PERSONALLY BY
HM THE QUEEN, IS PROUDLY WORN ON THE TUNIC OF
THIS MEMBER OF THE ROYAL MEWS.

*'I find it very heartening that
in this day and age, whilst
many of his contemporaries do
otherwise, the young trooper is
prepared to put such an
enormous amount of effort
and energy into the
preparation for a parade, and
takes enormous pride in
perfection both of turn-out and
drill, just as his father and
grandfather did before him.'*

Maj Sir Michael Parker KCVO,
CBE, talking about the Golden
Jubilee.

'All the horses that were to perform at the Jubilee were given special sound training for two weeks before the ceremonies. Early in the morning, the members of the mounted regiment who weren't going to be riding on the day were asked to become Rent-a-Crowd, along with their wives and families. We went out into Hyde Park and everyone made as much noise as they could, banging dustbins and shouting so that the horses could get used to the sounds that the mass crowds were going to make on the day of the Jubilee. At the beginning they kept bucking and bolting, trying to get away from the hullabaloo. But after the two weeks, they'd got used to it. On the Jubilee day, they mostly kept calm and were level headed. But nothing prepared us troopers for how thunderous and intense the noise was. I think we were less ready than the horses. The Jubilee had six divisions instead of the usual four. We had to bring in horses and troopers from everywhere!'

L/Cpl Douglas Eames

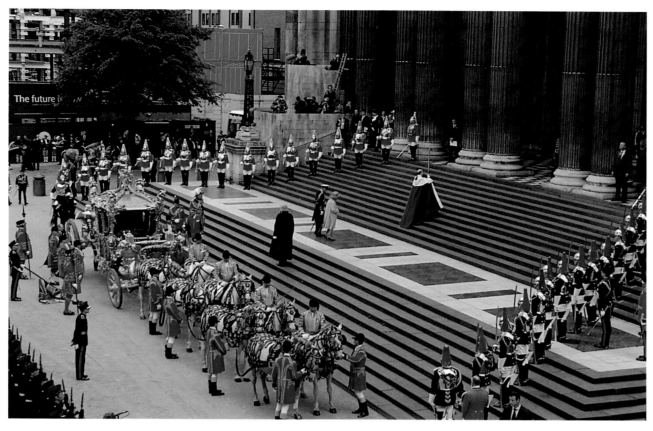

HER MAJESTY THE QUEEN WITH
HRH THE DUKE OF EDINBURGH
AND THE LORD MAYOR OF
LONDON, RT. HONOURABLE
ALDERMAN M. OLIVER, OUTSIDE
ST. PAUL'S CATHEDRAL FOR THE
GOLDEN JUBLIEE SERVICE

The Household Cavalry has three types of horses—drum horses (Clydesdale crosses, piebald or skewbald, usually named after Greek heroes); greys, ridden by trumpeters; and blacks. The Queen takes a keen interest in the drum horses and has bred horses for the regiment for this purpose. They must be of good temperament, well developed, at least 16.3 hands high, strong and fit enough to carry the considerable weight required. The blacks and the greys are virtually all unbroken Irish stock of three to four years old, at least 16.0 hands high. Unlike the drum horses, the naming of other horses is by way of a letter for each year. For identification purposes all the horses carry army and squadron numbers and regimental initials on their hooves.

THE KING'S TROOP ROYAL
HORSE ARTILLERY WHO ARE
HOUSEHOLD TROOPS PARTICIPATE
IN SOME CEREMONIAL EVENTS
ALONGSIDE THE HOUSEHOLD
CAVALRY

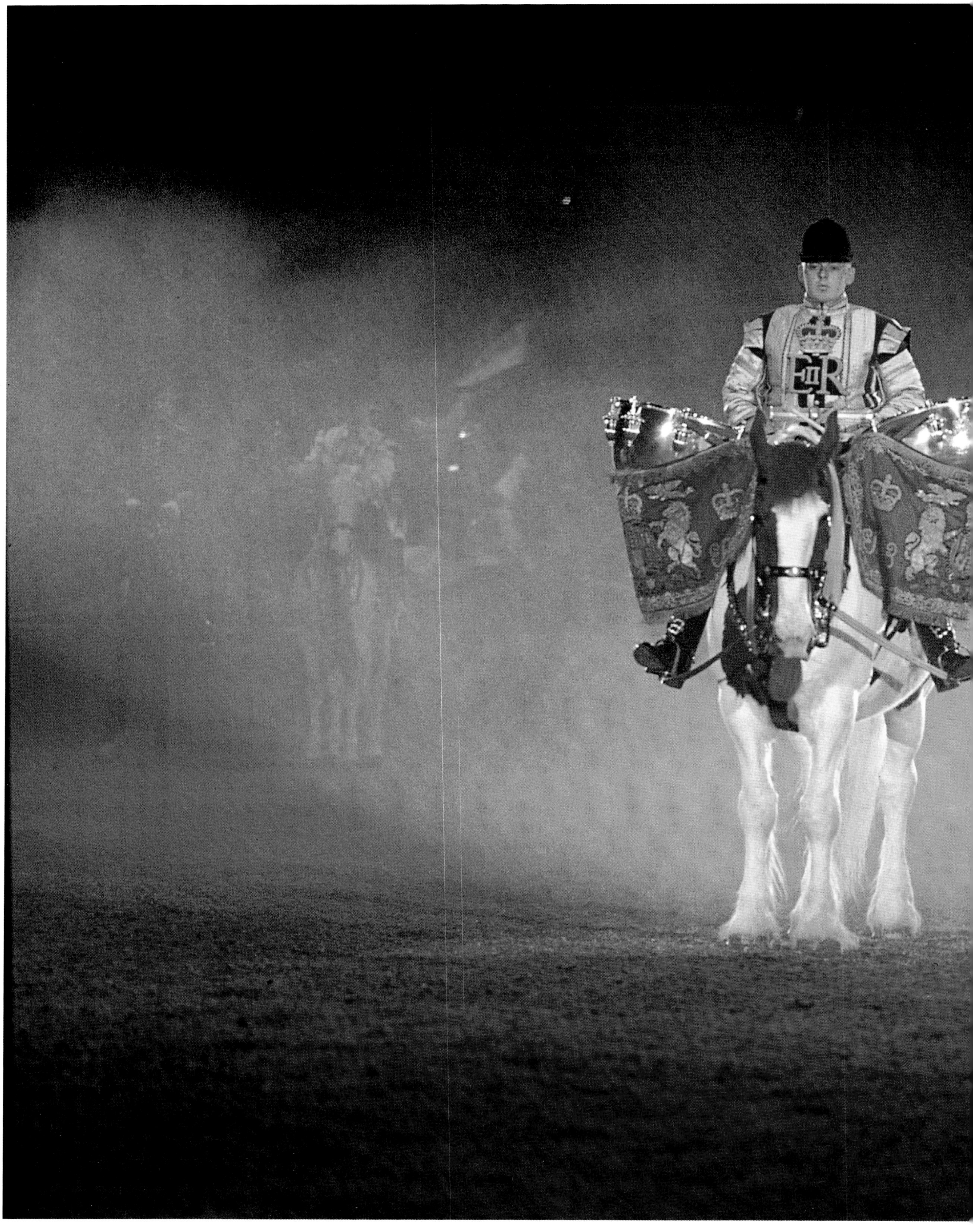

"This book is the culmination of six years spent photographing a subject that is both a symbol and an embodiment of British excellence. It has been a hugely rewarding and colourful experience as I come to understand the circle of tradition, endeavour and dedication, which revolves around the Household Cavalry. The Royal Family and the British people have together created a proud environment in which they unite in a superb and ongoing tradition."

Henry Dallal

Abbreviations

Military ranks have been abbreviated as follows:

Tpr	Trooper		
L/Cpl	Lance Corporal	CVRT	Combat Vehicle Reconnaissaince, Tracked
L/CoH	Lance Corporal of Horse (Corporal elsewhere in the Army)	DCM	Distinguished Conduct Medal
		GCB	Knight Grand Cross of the Order of the Bath
CoH	Corporal of Horse (Sergeant elsewhere in the Army)	GCVO	Knight Grand Cross of the Royal Victorian Order
Sgt	Sergeant	HM	Her (His) Majesty
WO2	Warrant Officer Class 2	HRH	Her (His) Royal Highness
WO1	Warrant Officer Class 1	KG	Knight of the Order of the Garter
GSM	Garrison Sergeant Major	KCVO	Knight Commander of the Royal Victorian Order
RCM	Regimental Corporal Major		
Lt	Lieutenant	LVO	Lieutenant of the Royal Victorian Order
Capt	Captain	MBE	Member of the Order of the British Empire
Maj	Major	MVO	Member of the Royal Victorian Order
Col	Colonel	OBE	Officer of the Order of the British Empire
Gen	General	QSO	Queen's Service Order
		RCMP	Royal Canadian Mounted Police

Other abbreviations

CB	Commander of the Order of the Bath
CBE	Commander of the Order of the British Empire